If Lost, Please Return To:

Name: _____

Phone: _____

Email: _____

Dedication

This Cocktail Recipes Journal is dedicated to all the people out there who want to keep track of their favorite cocktail recipes and document their findings in the process.

You are my inspiration for producing books and I'm honored to be a part of keeping all of your cocktail recipes, notes, and records organized.

This journal notebook will help you record your details about tracking your cocktail recipes.

Thoughtfully put together with these sections to record: Table of Contents, Cocktail Name, Equipment & Glass, Method, Ingredients, & Notes.

How to Use this Book

The purpose of this book is to keep all of your Cocktail Recipes notes all in one place. It will help keep you organized.

This Cocktail Recipes Journal will allow you to accurately document every detail about your cocktail recipes.

Here are examples of the prompts for you to fill in and write about your experience in this book:

1. Table of Contents - Easily find which page the cocktail recipe is on.

2. Cocktail Name - Write the name of the cocktail.

3. Equipment & Glass Required - Log any equipment or special glass needed.

4. Method - Record the process used to mix.

5. Ingredients Used - Log the ingredients used.

6. Notes - Ideal for recording ratios, mixes, instructions, alcohol content, servings, ideal occasion, ideal garnish, ideal glass or any other important information you want.

Table of Contents

Page	Cocktail Name
1	
2	
3	
4	
5	
6	
7	
8	
9	
10	
11	
12	
13	
14	
15	
16	
17	
18	
19	
20	

Table of Contents

Page	Cocktail Name
21	
22	
23	
24	
25	
26	
27	
28	
29	
30	
31	
32	
33	
34	
35	
36	
37	
38	
39	
40	

Table of Contents

Page	Cocktail name
41	
42	
43	
44	
45	
46	
47	
48	
49	
50	
51	
52	
53	
54	
55	
56	
57	
58	
59	
60	

Table of Contents

Page	Cocktail Name
61	
62	
63	
64	
65	
66	
67	
68	
69	
70	
71	
72	
73	
74	
75	
76	
77	
78	
79	
80	

Table of Contents

Page	Cocktail Name
81	
82	
83	
84	
85	
86	
87	
88	
89	
90	
91	
92	
93	
94	
95	
96	
97	
98	
99	
100	

COCKTAILS

PAGE	NAME
1	

INGREDIENTS

EQUIPMENT/GLASS REQUIRED

METHOD

NOTES

COCKTAILS

PAGE	NAME
2	

Ingredients

Equipment/Glass Required

Method

Notes

COCKTAILS

PAGE	NAME
3	

INGREDIENTS

EQUIPMENT/GLASS REQUIRED

METHOD

NOTES

COCKTAILS

PAGE	NAME
4	

INGREDIENTS

EQUIPMENT/GLASS REQUIRED

METHOD

NOTES

COCKTAILS

PAGE	NAME
5	

INGREDIENTS

EQUIPMENT/GLASS REQUIRED

METHOD

NOTES

COCKTAILS

PAGE	NAME
6	

INGREDIENTS

EQUIPMENT/GLASS REQUIRED

METHOD

NOTES

COCKTAILS

PAGE	NAME
7	

INGREDIENTS

EQUIPMENT / GLASS REQUIRED

METHOD

NOTES

COCKTAILS

PAGE	NAME
8	

Ingredients

Equipment/glass required

Method

Notes

COCKTAILS

PAGE	NAME
9	

INGREDIENTS

EQUIPMENT/GLASS REQUIRED

METHOD

NOTES

COCKTAILS

PAGE	NAME
10	

INGREDIENTS

EQUIPMENT/GLASS REQUIRED

METHOD

NOTES

COCKTAILS

PAGE	NAME
11	

INGREDIENTS

EQUIPMENT/GLASS REQUIRED

METHOD

NOTES

COCKTAILS

Page	Name
12	

Ingredients

Equipment/Glass Required

Method

Notes

COCKTAILS

PAGE	NAME
13	

INGREDIENTS

EQUIPMENT / GLASS REQUIRED

METHOD

NOTES

COCKTAILS

PAGE	NAME
14	

INGREDIENTS

EQUIPMENT/GLASS REQUIRED

METHOD

NOTES

COCKTAILS

PAGE	NAME
15	

INGREDIENTS

EQUIPMENT/GLASS REQUIRED

METHOD

NOTES

COCKTAILS

PAGE	NAME
16	

INGREDIENTS

EQUIPMENT/GLASS REQUIRED

METHOD

NOTES

COCKTAILS

PAGE	NAME
17	

INGREDIENTS

EQUIPMENT/GLASS REQUIRED

METHOD

NOTES

COCKTAILS

PAGE	NAME
18	

INGREDIENTS

EQUIPMENT/GLASS REQUIRED

METHOD

NOTES

COCKTAILS

PAGE	NAME
19	

INGREDIENTS

EQUIPMENT/GLASS REQUIRED

METHOD

NOTES

COCKTAILS

PAGE	NAME
20	

Ingredients

Equipment/glass required

Method

Notes

COCKTAILS

Page: 21

COCKTAILS

PAGE	NAME
22	

Ingredients

Equipment/glass required

Method

Notes

COCKTAILS

PAGE	NAME
23	

INGREDIENTS

EQUIPMENT/GLASS REQUIRED

METHOD

NOTES

COCKTAILS

PAGE	NAME
24	

INGREDIENTS

EQUIPMENT/GLASS REQUIRED

METHOD

NOTES

COCKTAILS

PAGE	NAME
25	

INGREDIENTS

EQUIPMENT/GLASS REQUIRED

METHOD

NOTES

COCKTAILS

PAGE	NAME
26	

INGREDIENTS

EQUIPMENT/GLASS REQUIRED

METHOD

NOTES

COCKTAILS

PAGE	NAME
27	

INGREDIENTS

EQUIPMENT/GLASS REQUIRED

METHOD

NOTES

COCKTAILS

PAGE	NAME
28	

Ingredients

Equipment/Glass Required

Method

Notes

COCKTAILS

PAGE	NAME
29	

INGREDIENTS

EQUIPMENT/GLASS REQUIRED

METHOD

NOTES

COCKTAILS

PAGE	NAME
30	

Ingredients

Equipment/glass required

Method

Notes

COCKTAILS

PAGE	NAME
31	

INGREDIENTS

EQUIPMENT/GLASS REQUIRED

METHOD

NOTES

COCKTAILS

PAGE	NAME
32	

Ingredients

Equipment/Glass required

Method

Notes

COCKTAILS

PAGE	NAME
33	

INGREDIENTS

EQUIPMENT/GLASS REQUIRED

METHOD

NOTES

COCKTAILS

PAGE	NAME
34	

Ingredients

Equipment/glass required

Method

Notes

COCKTAILS

PAGE	NAME
35	

INGREDIENTS

EQUIPMENT/GLASS REQUIRED

METHOD

NOTES

COCKTAILS

PAGE	NAME
36	

INGREDIENTS

EQUIPMENT/GLASS REQUIRED

METHOD

NOTES

COCKTAILS

PAGE	NAME
37	

INGREDIENTS

EQUIPMENT / GLASS REQUIRED

METHOD

NOTES

COCKTAILS

PAGE: 38

NAME:

INGREDIENTS

EQUIPMENT/GLASS REQUIRED

METHOD

NOTES

COCKTAILS

PAGE	NAME
39	

INGREDIENTS

EQUIPMENT/GLASS REQUIRED

METHOD

NOTES

COCKTAILS

PAGE	NAME
40	

Ingredients

Equipment/Glass required

Method

Notes

COCKTAILS

PAGE	NAME
41	

INGREDIENTS

EQUIPMENT/GLASS REQUIRED

METHOD

NOTES

COCKTAILS

PAGE	NAME
42	

INGREDIENTS

EQUIPMENT/GLASS REQUIRED

METHOD

NOTES

COCKTAILS

PAGE	NAME
43	

INGREDIENTS

EQUIPMENT / GLASS REQUIRED

METHOD

NOTES

COCKTAILS

PAGE	NAME
44	

Ingredients

Equipment/Glass required

Method

Notes

COCKTAILS

PAGE	NAME
45	

INGREDIENTS

EQUIPMENT/GLASS REQUIRED

METHOD

NOTES

COCKTAILS

PAGE	NAME
46	

INGREDIENTS

EQUIPMENT/GLASS REQUIRED

METHOD

NOTES

COCKTAILS

PAGE	NAME
47	

INGREDIENTS

EQUIPMENT/GLASS REQUIRED

METHOD

NOTES

COCKTAILS

PAGE	NAME
48	

Ingredients

Equipment/Glass Required

Method

Notes

COCKTAILS

PAGE	NAME
49	

INGREDIENTS

EQUIPMENT/GLASS REQUIRED

METHOD

NOTES

COCKTAILS

PAGE	NAME
50	

Ingredients

Equipment/glass required

Method

Notes

COCKTAILS

PAGE	NAME
51	

INGREDIENTS

EQUIPMENT/GLASS REQUIRED

METHOD

NOTES

COCKTAILS

PAGE	NAME
52	

INGREDIENTS

EQUIPMENT/GLASS REQUIRED

METHOD

NOTES

COCKTAILS

PAGE	NAME
53	

INGREDIENTS

EQUIPMENT/GLASS REQUIRED

METHOD

NOTES

COCKTAILS

Page	Name
54	

Ingredients

Equipment/Glass required

Method

Notes

COCKTAILS

PAGE	NAME
55	

INGREDIENTS

EQUIPMENT/GLASS REQUIRED

METHOD

NOTES

COCKTAILS

PAGE	NAME
56	

Ingredients

Equipment/Glass Required

Method

Notes

COCKTAILS

PAGE	NAME
57	

INGREDIENTS

EQUIPMENT/GLASS REQUIRED

METHOD

NOTES

COCKTAILS

PAGE	NAME
58	

Ingredients

Equipment/Glass required

Method

Notes

COCKTAILS

PAGE	NAME
59	

INGREDIENTS

EQUIPMENT / GLASS REQUIRED

METHOD

NOTES

COCKTAILS

PAGE	NAME
60	

INGREDIENTS

EQUIPMENT/GLASS REQUIRED

METHOD

NOTES

COCKTAILS

PAGE	NAME
61	

INGREDIENTS

EQUIPMENT/GLASS REQUIRED

METHOD

NOTES

COCKTAILS

PAGE	NAME
62	

Ingredients

Equipment/glass required

Method

Notes

COCKTAILS

PAGE	NAME
63	

INGREDIENTS

EQUIPMENT/GLASS REQUIRED

METHOD

NOTES

COCKTAILS

PAGE	NAME
64	

INGREDIENTS

EQUIPMENT/GLASS REQUIRED

METHOD

NOTES

COCKTAILS

PAGE	NAME
65	

INGREDIENTS

EQUIPMENT / GLASS REQUIRED

METHOD

NOTES

COCKTAILS

PAGE	NAME
66	

Ingredients

Equipment/Glass Required

Method

Notes

COCKTAILS

PAGE	NAME
67	

INGREDIENTS

EQUIPMENT/GLASS REQUIRED

METHOD

NOTES

COCKTAILS

PAGE	NAME
68	

INGREDIENTS

EQUIPMENT/GLASS REQUIRED

METHOD

NOTES

COCKTAILS

PAGE: 69

NAME:

INGREDIENTS

EQUIPMENT/GLASS REQUIRED

METHOD

NOTES

COCKTAILS

Page	Name
70	

Ingredients

Equipment/Glass required

Method

Notes

COCKTAILS

PAGE	NAME
71	

INGREDIENTS

EQUIPMENT/GLASS REQUIRED

METHOD

NOTES

COCKTAILS

PAGE	NAME
72	

INGREDIENTS

EQUIPMENT/GLASS REQUIRED

METHOD

NOTES

COCKTAILS

PAGE	NAME
73	

INGREDIENTS

EQUIPMENT/GLASS REQUIRED

METHOD

NOTES

COCKTAILS

PAGE	NAME
74	

Ingredients

Equipment/Glass required

Method

Notes

COCKTAILS

PAGE	NAME
75	

INGREDIENTS

EQUIPMENT/GLASS REQUIRED

METHOD

NOTES

COCKTAILS

PAGE: 76

NAME:

INGREDIENTS:

EQUIPMENT/GLASS REQUIRED:

METHOD:

NOTES:

COCKTAILS

PAGE	NAME
77	

INGREDIENTS

EQUIPMENT/GLASS REQUIRED

METHOD

NOTES

COCKTAILS

PAGE	NAME
78	

INGREDIENTS

EQUIPMENT/GLASS REQUIRED

METHOD

NOTES

COCKTAILS

PAGE	NAME
79	

INGREDIENTS

EQUIPMENT/GLASS REQUIRED

METHOD

NOTES

COCKTAILS

PAGE	NAME
80	

INGREDIENTS

EQUIPMENT/GLASS REQUIRED

METHOD

NOTES

COCKTAILS

PAGE	NAME
81	

INGREDIENTS

EQUIPMENT/GLASS REQUIRED

METHOD

NOTES

COCKTAILS

PAGE	NAME
82	

INGREDIENTS

EQUIPMENT/GLASS REQUIRED

METHOD

NOTES

COCKTAILS

PAGE	NAME
83	

INGREDIENTS

EQUIPMENT/GLASS REQUIRED

METHOD

NOTES

COCKTAILS

PAGE	NAME
84	

INGREDIENTS

EQUIPMENT/GLASS REQUIRED

METHOD

NOTES

COCKTAILS

PAGE	NAME
85	

INGREDIENTS

EQUIPMENT/GLASS REQUIRED

METHOD

NOTES

COCKTAILS

PAGE	NAME
86	

Ingredients

Equipment/glass required

Method

Notes

COCKTAILS

PAGE	NAME
87	

INGREDIENTS

EQUIPMENT/GLASS REQUIRED

METHOD

NOTES

COCKTAILS

PAGE	NAME
88	

INGREDIENTS

EQUIPMENT/GLASS REQUIRED

METHOD

NOTES

COCKTAILS

PAGE	NAME
89	

INGREDIENTS

EQUIPMENT/GLASS REQUIRED

METHOD

NOTES

COCKTAILS

PAGE	NAME
90	

Ingredients

Equipment/Glass required

Method

Notes

COCKTAILS

PAGE	NAME
91	

INGREDIENTS

EQUIPMENT/GLASS REQUIRED

METHOD

NOTES

COCKTAILS

PAGE	NAME
92	

Ingredients

Equipment/glass required

Method

Notes

COCKTAILS

PAGE	NAME
93	

INGREDIENTS

EQUIPMENT/GLASS REQUIRED

METHOD

NOTES

COCKTAILS

PAGE	NAME
94	

INGREDIENTS

EQUIPMENT/GLASS REQUIRED

METHOD

NOTES

COCKTAILS

PAGE	NAME
95	

INGREDIENTS

EQUIPMENT/GLASS REQUIRED

METHOD

NOTES

COCKTAILS

PAGE	NAME
96	

Ingredients

Equipment/glass required

Method

Notes

COCKTAILS

PAGE	NAME
97	

INGREDIENTS

EQUIPMENT/GLASS REQUIRED

METHOD

NOTES

COCKTAILS

PAGE: 98

NAME:

Ingredients

Equipment/glass required

Method

Notes

COCKTAILS

PAGE	NAME
99	

INGREDIENTS

EQUIPMENT/GLASS REQUIRED

METHOD

NOTES

COCKTAILS

PAGE	NAME
100	

Ingredients

Equipment/Glass required

Method

Notes

www.ingramcontent.com/pod-product-compliance
Lightning Source LLC
Chambersburg PA
CBHW071402080526
44587CB00017B/3160